GRAPHIC MYTHOLOGY

ROMAN MYTHS

by David West

illustrated by Ross Watton

The Rosen Publishing Group, Inc., New York

Published in 2006 by The Rosen Publishing Group, Inc.
29 East 21st Street, New York, NY 10010

First edition, 2006

Designed and produced by
David West Books

Editor: Kate Newport

Photo credits:
Pages 4/5 (middle), Buckaroo
Page 5 (bottom), mlane
Page 6 (top), Sue Colvil and Bart Parren

Library of Congress Cataloging-in-Publication Data

West, David.
  Roman myths / by David West ; illustrated by Ross Watton.
    p. cm. -- (Graphic mythology)
  Includes index.
  ISBN 1-4042-0803-8 (library binding) -- ISBN 1-4042-0815-1 (pbk.) -- ISBN 1-4042-6255-5 (6 pack)
  1. Mythology, Roman. I. Watton, Ross. II. Title. III. Series.
  BL803.W47 2005
  292.1'3--dc22

                                      2005017223

Manufactured in China

CONTENTS

THE ROMAN WORLD

The Romans were a very superstitious people, and they worshipped many gods and goddesses. Most of their gods and myths were based on Greek beliefs. However, the Romans gave the gods their own names.

TEMPLES AND WORSHIP

The Romans built many temples dedicated to their gods. Roman people would pray at these temples. They would also leave presents to encourage the gods to hear their prayers. Sometimes, the Romans would visit a special priest or priestess, called an oracle, to learn what would happen in the future. As the Roman empire grew, many foreign gods and myths became popular. The Persian god Mithras was worshipped by Roman soldiers because they felt he could give life after death to those who had died bravely in battle.

AT HOME

Romans believed that there were holy spirits that lived in the home and in the land that needed to be kept happy. Most Romans had their own small shrine or holy area in their homes where they could pray every day. They would leave offerings of wine, cakes, and spices.

Faunus was the god of shepherds who also told the future. He had the head and chest of a man, and the legs of a goat.

ROMAN	GREEK
NAMES:	NAMES:
Jupiter	Zeus
Juno	Hera
Minerva	Athena
Pluto	Hades
Neptune	Poseidon
Bacchus	Dionysus
Diana	Diana
Venus	Aphrodite
Apollo	Apollo
Ceres	Demeter
Mars	Ares
Vulcan	Hephaestus
Cupid	Eros
Mercury	Hermes

Roman temples like this one in Sicily were copied from Greek temples.

Neptune was the brother of Jupiter, the king of the gods. Jupiter gave Neptune the sea as his kingdom.

The main spirit of one's house was Genius. He was worshipped by everyone, including the slaves. There was also Lares, who protected the household, and Penates, who looked after the store cupboard and all the food and drink in it. There were also State Lares who protected the Roman nation and were celebrated in public ceremonies. Even the emperor was worshipped as the State Genius. Many emperors were made into gods when they died.

THREE ROMAN MYTHS

Although many of the Roman myths are based on ancient Greek myths, there are some that originated in Rome. The three stories in this book are all real Roman myths.

Ancient Romans believed that Rome was built by Romulus.

AENEAS' JOURNEY

The Romans thought their empire was started by a Trojan hero named Aeneas. It is a story of an epic journey to find a new home for the defeated people of Troy. Aeneas was the son of Anchises, a human, and Venus, the goddess of love, and because of this many of the gods wanted to help him in his journey.

Aeneas
The son of Venus and Anchises.

Anchises
A Trojan man, who is father of Aeneas.

Apollo
The god of the sun, healing, and music.

Dido
The queen of Carthage, North Africa.

Lavinia
The daughter of King Latinus who marries Aeneas.

Sibyl
A prophetess who lives in a cave at Cumae, Italy.

Turnus
The king of the Rutulians.

Venus
The goddess of love and mother of Aeneas.

ROMULUS AND REMUS

The name Rome came from the most famous of all Roman myths, the story of Romulus and Remus. It tells of what happens to the twins as they grow up, and the hatred and murder that finally leads to the building of Rome.

Amulius
The jealous brother of Numitor.

Numitor
The ruler of Alba Longa and grand-father to the twins.

Rhea Silvia
The daughter of Numitor and mother of Romulus and Remus.

Remus
The twin brother of Romulus.

Romulus
The twin brother of Remus and the founder of Rome.

HERO HORATIUS

The Romans loved stories of heroic deeds. The story of Horatius Cocles has been shown in paintings and poems ever since early Roman times. Long ago, the people of Rome were under attack from other tribes, including the Etruscan people in the north. In one battle, Lars Porsena, an Etruscan, attacked Rome with a huge army, and all that stood between Rome and its invaders was Horatius and a bridge.

Horatius Cocles
The Roman soldier who defends a bridge against the Etruscans.

Spurius Lartius
A Roman soldier who helps Horatius defend the bridge.

Titus Herminius
A second Roman soldier who helps Horatius defend the bridge.

THE WANDERINGS OF AENEAS
(ANCESTOR OF THE ROMANS)

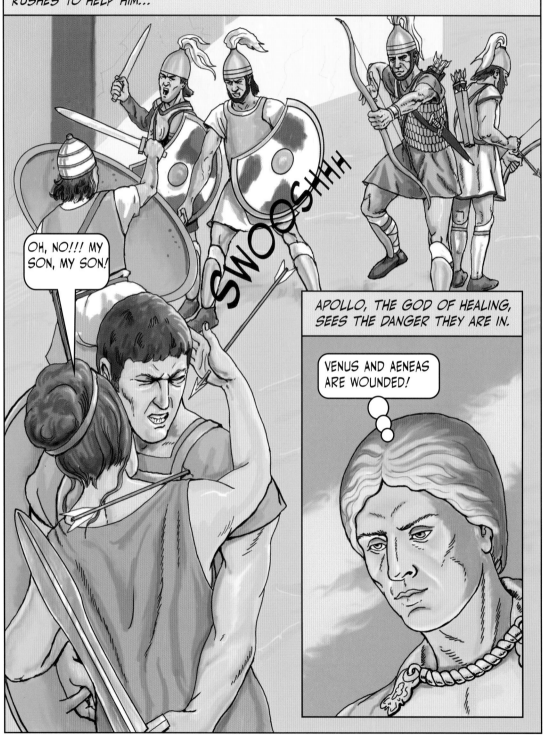

AFTER NINE YEARS, THE SIEGE OF TROY WAS STILL GOING. WHILE DEFENDING THE CITY, AENEAS IS WOUNDED BY DIOMEDES. AENEAS' MOTHER, THE GODDESS VENUS, RUSHES TO HELP HIM...

SWOOSHHH

OH, NO!!! MY SON, MY SON!

APOLLO, THE GOD OF HEALING, SEES THE DANGER THEY ARE IN.

VENUS AND AENEAS ARE WOUNDED!

APOLLO SHIELDS THEM FROM THE FLYING ARROWS.

CLANG

AS HE TAKES THEM AWAY, APOLLO LEAVES BEHIND A COPY OF AENEAS TO FOOL HIS GREEK ENEMIES.

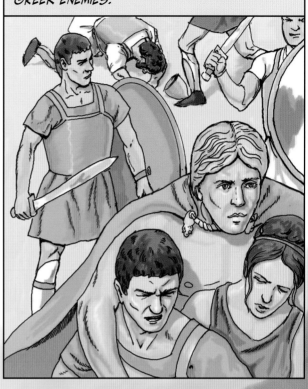

IN THE TEMPLE OF APOLLO, ARTEMIS AND LETO HEAL AENEAS OF HIS WOUNDS.

SOON, AENEAS IS STRONG ENOUGH TO CONTINUE FIGHTING.

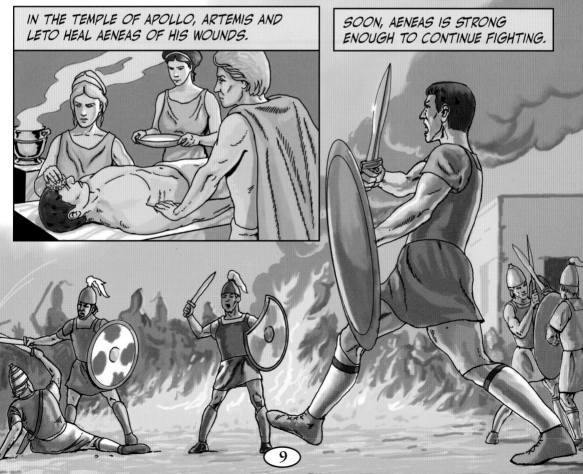

USING THE WOODEN TROJAN HORSE, THE GREEKS DEFEAT THE CITY OF TROY.

I WILL HOLD THEM BACK WHILE YOU ESCAPE!

AENEAS HELPS THE SURVIVORS ESCAPE.

SEEING HE CAN DO NO MORE, AENEAS LEAVES TROY CARRYING HIS FATHER ON HIS BACK.

LET HIM GO. HE IS HELPING AN OLD MAN.

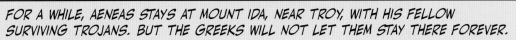

FOR A WHILE, AENEAS STAYS AT MOUNT IDA, NEAR TROY, WITH HIS FELLOW SURVIVING TROJANS. BUT THE GREEKS WILL NOT LET THEM STAY THERE FOREVER.

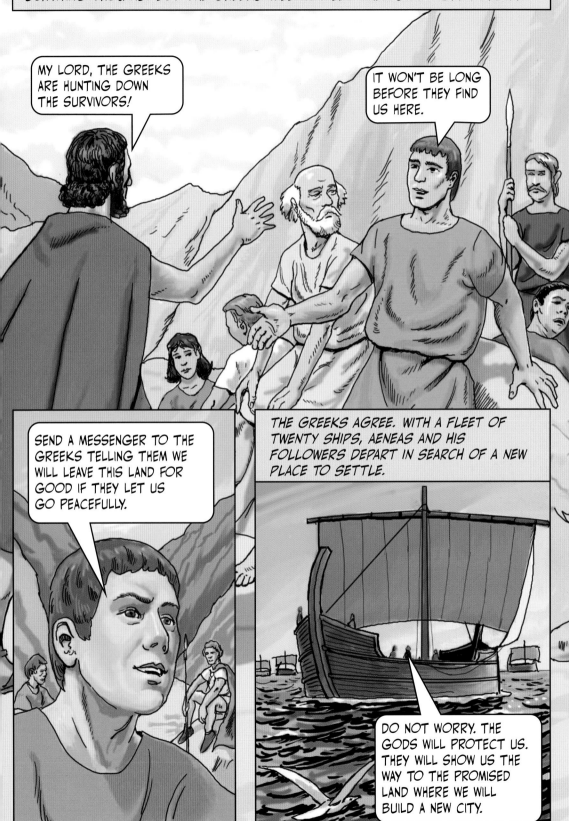

MY LORD, THE GREEKS ARE HUNTING DOWN THE SURVIVORS!

IT WON'T BE LONG BEFORE THEY FIND US HERE.

SEND A MESSENGER TO THE GREEKS TELLING THEM WE WILL LEAVE THIS LAND FOR GOOD IF THEY LET US GO PEACEFULLY.

THE GREEKS AGREE. WITH A FLEET OF TWENTY SHIPS, AENEAS AND HIS FOLLOWERS DEPART IN SEARCH OF A NEW PLACE TO SETTLE.

DO NOT WORRY. THE GODS WILL PROTECT US. THEY WILL SHOW US THE WAY TO THE PROMISED LAND WHERE WE WILL BUILD A NEW CITY.

THE FIRST STOP ON THEIR VOYAGE IS THRACE. SUDDENLY, A GHOST APPEARS BEFORE AENEAS!

GET AWAY FROM THIS CRUEL LAND!

WHO ARE YOU?

I AM POLYDORUS, KING OF THRACE. POLYMESTOR MURDERED ME. LEAVE THESE SHORES FOR YOUR OWN SAFETY.

AENEAS LEAVES THRACE AND SAILS ON TO CRETE. THE SHIPS ANCHOR, AND AENEAS IS GREETED KINDLY BY KING ANIUS. THEY DO NOT STAY LONG.

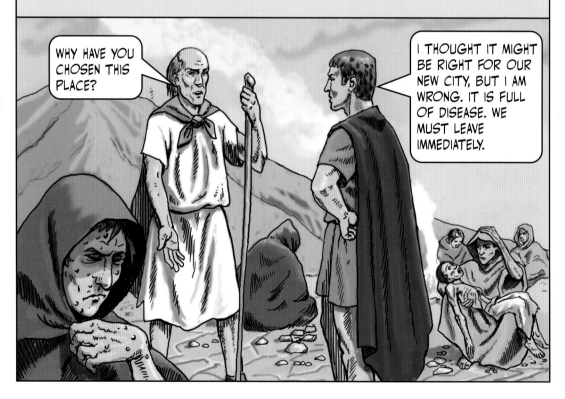

WHY HAVE YOU CHOSEN THIS PLACE?

I THOUGHT IT MIGHT BE RIGHT FOR OUR NEW CITY, BUT I AM WRONG. IT IS FULL OF DISEASE. WE MUST LEAVE IMMEDIATELY.

AS THEY LEAVE CRETE, THE GODS APPEAR BEFORE AENEAS.

...YOU MUST SAIL TO ITALY.

...SAIL TO ITALY.

...SAIL TO ITALY.

WHERE IS THIS ITALY?

GO TO BUTHROTUM. THERE YOU WILL FIND YOUR ANSWER.

YOU WILL NEVER FIND THE PLACE YOU SEEK. NOT UNTIL HUNGER FORCES YOU TO EAT THE TABLES YOUR FOOD IS ON!!!

ON THEIR WAY, THEY ARE ATTACKED BY WINGED MONSTERS - HARPIES.

13

IN BUTHROTUM, AENEAS IS GIVEN DIRECTIONS TO ITALY BY HELENUS. THEY THEN SET OFF ONCE AGAIN BUT THE GODDESS JUNO SENDS A STORM THAT BLOWS THE SHIPS OFF COURSE...

THEY EVENTUALLY END UP AT A BEAUTIFUL CITY CALLED CARTHAGE IN NORTH AFRICA.

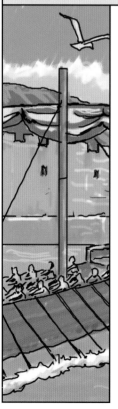

THIS REALLY IS WONDERFUL.

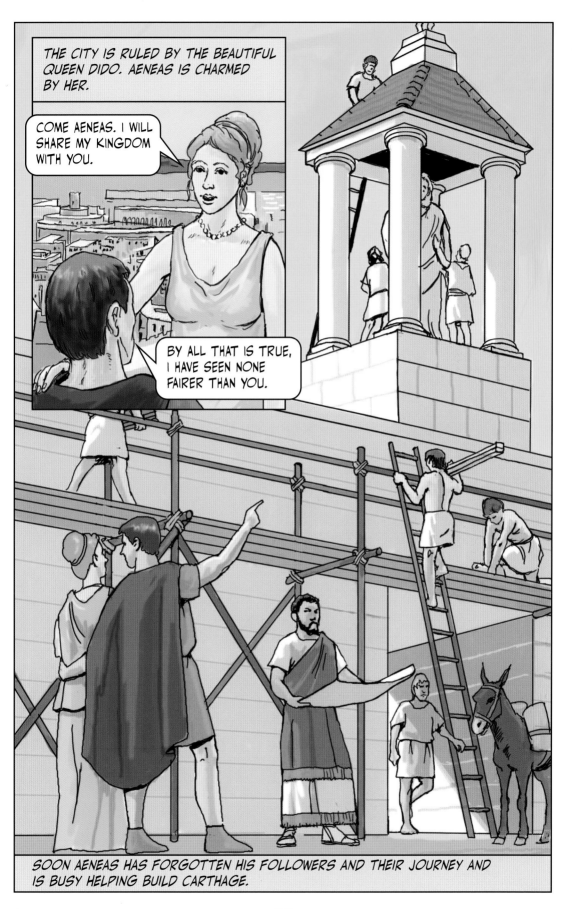

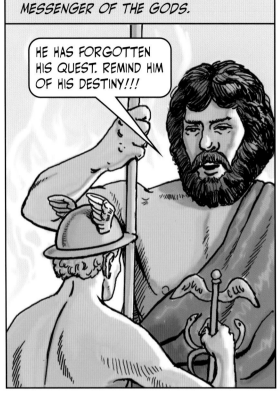

JUPITER, THE CHIEF GOD, WATCHES AENEAS AND CALLS FOR MERCURY, THE MESSENGER OF THE GODS.

HE HAS FORGOTTEN HIS QUEST. REMIND HIM OF HIS DESTINY!!!

NOW YOU ARE BUILDING CARTHAGE TO PLEASE A WOMAN? WHAT HAS HAPPENED TO YOUR JOURNEY?

YOU ARE RIGHT. I MUST LEAVE DIDO AND LEAD MY PEOPLE.

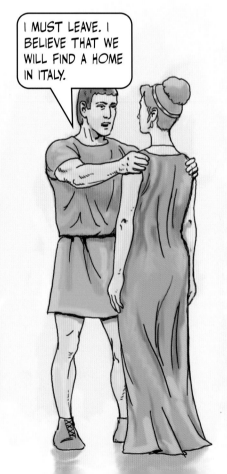

I MUST LEAVE. I BELIEVE THAT WE WILL FIND A HOME IN ITALY.

16

AENEAS GATHERS HIS FOLLOWERS FROM THE CITY AND SETS SAIL FOR ITALY.

DIDO CANNOT BEAR THE SEPARATION. IN HER GRIEF SHE DIES, FLINGING HERSELF INTO A FIRE.

FROM HIS SHIP, AENEAS SEES A FIRE BURNING BRIGHTLY ON A TOWER HIGH ABOVE THE WALLS OF CARTHAGE.

FATHER, YOU LOOK ILL!

AYE, MY SON. MY TIME IS NEARLY UP. IT IS ONLY TO BE EXPECTED OF SOMEONE MY AGE.

BEFORE LONG, AENEAS' FATHER PEACEFULLY DIES. THE FLEET STOP AT DREPANUM, SICILY, FOR ANCHISES' FUNERAL. HE IS BURIED AT THE FOOT OF A MOUNTAIN.

FROM NOW ON, LET THIS MOUNTAIN BE KNOWN AS ANCHISIA.

AFTER THE FUNERAL, AENEAS SETS SAIL ONCE MORE AND FINALLY LANDS ON THE ITALIAN COAST AT CUMAE. HERE HE SEARCHES FOR A GUIDE TO THE UNDERWORLD.

I AM TOLD THE SIBYL LIVES IN A CAVE NEAR HERE.

TELL ME, SIBYL, IS IT TRUE THAT THE GATE TO THE UNDERWORLD IS HERE?

I WISH TO SEE MY FATHER ONCE MORE.

I WILL TAKE YOU TO HIM.

BUT FIRST, YOU MUST PICK A GOLDEN BOUGH FROM THE SACRED GROVE TO LIGHT OUR WAY.

WHEN AENEAS RETURNS WITH THE BOUGH, THE SIBYL LEADS HIM THROUGH A GATE INTO THE UNDERWORLD.

CHARON, THE FERRYMAN, TAKES THEM ACROSS THE RIVER STYX.

SUDDENLY, AENEAS SEES DIDO!

OH NO, DIDO! YOU CAN'T BE DEAD?

...SHE TURNS HER BACK ON HIM.

AENEAS PASSES THOSE BEING PUNISHED FOR THEIR SINS.

FINALLY THEY REACH THE SACRED MEADOWS OF ELYSIUM...

FATHER!

HUH?

...BUT HIS FATHER IS A MISTY SHADOW WHO CANNOT BE HELD.

LET ME SHOW YOU THE FUTURE.

WHO ARE THEY?

THEY ARE CALLED THE ROMANS, AND THEY WILL CREATE A GREAT EMPIRE.

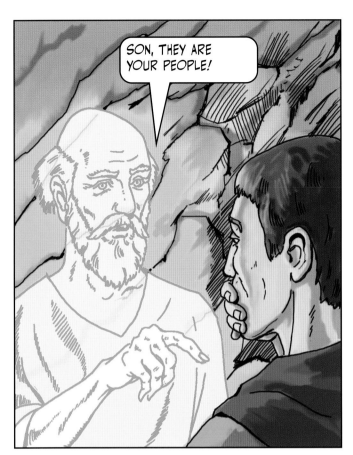

AENEAS AND THE SIBYL GO BACK THE WAY THEY CAME TO THE LAND OF THE LIVING...

THEIR SHIPS TRAVEL UP THE COAST AND STOP AT THE MOUTH OF THE TIBER RIVER.

LET'S GO ASHORE AND SET UP CAMP.

LATER, THEY ARE EATING THEIR DINNER OF MEAT ON SLICES OF WHEAT CAKE.

WHAT DID THE HARPIES SAY?

THAT WE WOULD ONLY FIND OUR HOME WHEN WE ATE THE TABLES OUR FOOD IS ON.

WELL, ARE WE NOT DOING JUST THAT?

YES, YOU'RE RIGHT. THIS WHEAT CAKE IS JUST LIKE A TABLE, AND THE MEAT IS FOOD ON TOP.

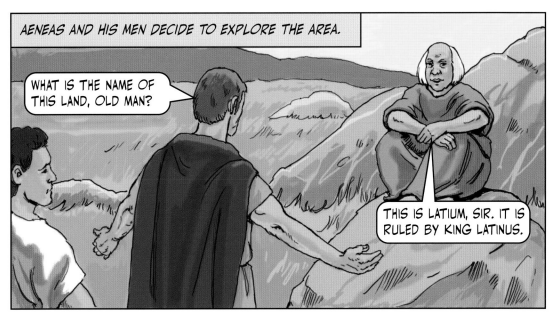

AENEAS AND HIS MEN DECIDE TO EXPLORE THE AREA.

WHAT IS THE NAME OF THIS LAND, OLD MAN?

THIS IS LATIUM, SIR. IT IS RULED BY KING LATINUS.

NEXT, AENEAS MEETS THE KING AND HIS DAUGHTER.

WE HAVE COME FROM TROY. I HAVE BEEN TOLD BY THE GODS TO BUILD A NEW CITY FOR MY PEOPLE.

YOU ARE WELCOME HERE, AENEAS. THERE ARE MANY PLACES TO BUILD A NEW CITY. BUT THERE ARE ALSO MANY TRIBES WHO WILL NOT TAKE KINDLY TO FOREIGNERS.

AENEAS FALLS IN LOVE WITH LAVINIA, THE KING'S DAUGHTER.

BUT SHE IS PROMISED TO KING TURNUS OF THE RUTULIANS.

THE ORACLE SAYS SHE WILL MARRY A FOREIGNER.

TELL TURNUS THAT THIS FOREIGNER WISHES TO STEAL HIS FUTURE BRIDE.

MY LORD, I ASK FOR YOUR DAUGHTER'S HAND IN MARRIAGE.

MY DEAR AENEAS, I WOULD LIKE NOTHING MORE. HOWEVER, WE HAVE A SLIGHT—SHALL WE SAY—PROBLEM...

AFTER THIS, AENEAS MARRIES LAVINIA. THE GODS ARE PLEASED WHEN WORK BEGINS ON A NEW CITY.

I WILL CALL THE NEW LAND LAVINIUM, AFTER ITS QUEEN.

AENEAS AND LAVINIA RULE FOR MANY YEARS...

...BUT THERE ARE ALWAYS ENEMIES TO FIGHT. SADLY, ONE DAY AENEAS IS KILLED IN A FIGHT WITH SOLDIERS OF MELENTIUS, AN OLD ALLY OF TURNUS'.

VENUS ASKS JUPITER TO MAKE AENEAS A GOD. JUPITER GRANTS HER REQUEST.

YOU SHALL BE WORSHIPPED AS INDIGES.

THE END

ROMULUS AND REMUS

KING NUMITOR IS A RELATIVE OF AENEAS. HE IS THE RULER OF ALBA LONGA, A CITY FOUNDED BY AENEAS' SON.

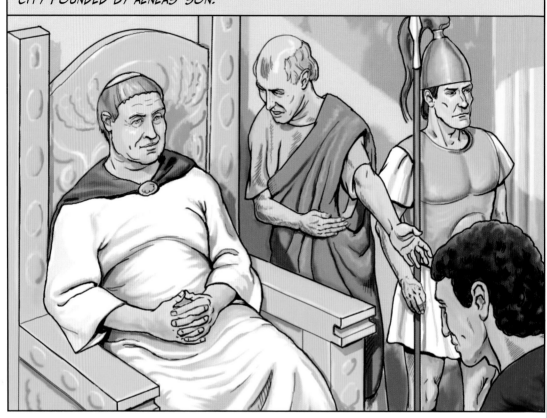

KING NUMITOR HAS A BROTHER CALLED AMULIUS, WHO IS JEALOUS OF HIM.

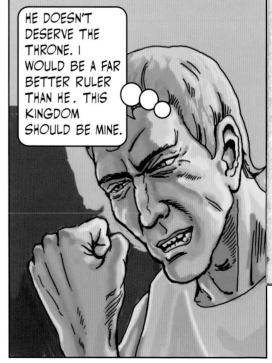

HE DOESN'T DESERVE THE THRONE. I WOULD BE A FAR BETTER RULER THAN HE. THIS KINGDOM SHOULD BE MINE.

AMULIUS GATHERS HIS FOLLOWERS AND THREATENS NUMITOR WITH HIS LIFE.

NUMITOR MANAGES TO ESCAPE AND LEAVES THE CITY.

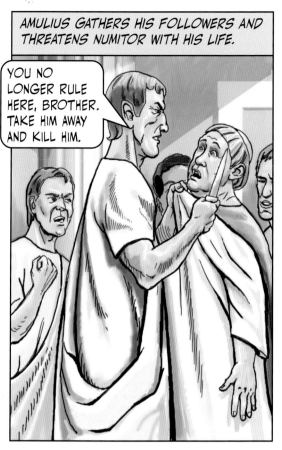

YOU NO LONGER RULE HERE, BROTHER. TAKE HIM AWAY AND KILL HIM.

AMULIUS IS NOW KING, BUT HE FEARS THAT GRANDSONS OF HIS BROTHER WILL ONE DAY TAKE THE THRONE FROM HIM. HE THINKS OF NUMITOR'S DAUGHTER, RHEA SILVIA.

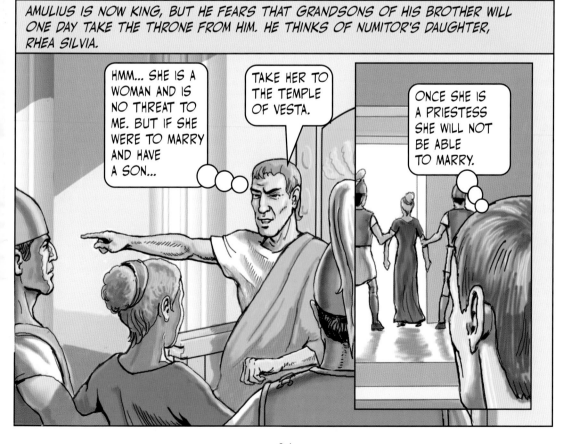

HMM... SHE IS A WOMAN AND IS NO THREAT TO ME. BUT IF SHE WERE TO MARRY AND HAVE A SON...

TAKE HER TO THE TEMPLE OF VESTA.

ONCE SHE IS A PRIESTESS SHE WILL NOT BE ABLE TO MARRY.

HOWEVER, AMULIUS' PLAN IS STOPPED. MARS, THE GOD OF WAR, SECRETLY VISITS RHEA SILVIA AND GIVES HER TWIN BOYS.

I SHALL CALL YOU ROMULUS. AND YOU SHALL BE REMUS.

WHAT?

TWINS?

BOYS?

KILL THEM! DROWN THEM IN THE TIBER!

AND THROW THEIR MOTHER IN PRISON!

32

NOOOO!

NOT MY BABIES!

I'M SORRY, MY LADY, I'M ONLY OBEYING ORDERS.

THE SERVANT GIVEN THE TASK OF DROWNING THE TWINS TAKES PITY ON THEM.

I SHALL LET THE GODS DECIDE YOUR FATE.

THE BASKET COMES TO REST ON THE GENTLY SLOPING BANKS NEAR THE SEVEN HILLS.

WAAHH!

A SHE-WOLF, WHOSE CUBS HAVE JUST DIED...

...FINDS THE TWINS IN THE BASKET...

GRRR!

WAAH WAAH

SHE TAKES CARE OF THEM.

34

A FEW DAYS LATER, FAUSTULUS, A SHEPHERD, FINDS THE BOYS. HE TAKES THEM HOME AND RAISES THEM AS IF THEY WERE HIS OWN.

IN TIME, THE BOYS GROW UP TO BE STRONG AND HEALTHY. THEY ARE BOTH BRAVE YOUNG MEN.

ONE DAY...

FAUSTULUS, WHO WAS OUR MOTHER?

IT IS SAID YOU ARE THE SONS OF RHEA SILVIA.

AMULIUS TRIED TO HAVE YOU KILLED. HE IMPRISONED YOUR MOTHER.

ONE DAY, WE WILL PUNISH AMULIUS FOR WHAT HE DID TO OUR MOTHER.

35

WHEN THEY ARE GROWN MEN, THE TWINS FORM A SMALL ARMY. THEY HAVE NEVER FORGOTTEN THEIR MOTHER'S SUFFERING. THEY ATTACK ALBA LONGA.

AMULIUS IS KILLED!!!

AAARGH!

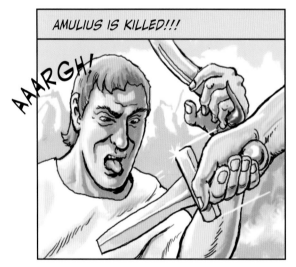

THE TWINS HAVE NUMITOR PUT BACK ON THE THRONE OF ALBA LONGA. ONCE AGAIN, ORDER IS RESTORED.

RELEASE OUR MOTHER FROM PRISON NOW!

ONE DAY, THE TWINS ARE WALKING NEAR THE SEVEN HILLS...

LET'S BUILD A CITY ON ONE OF THESE HILLS.

YES, BUT WHICH ONE?

THAT ONE IS THE OBVIOUS CHOICE.

I DISAGREE. THE ONE ON THE LEFT HAS HIGHER SLOPES!

ONLY ONE OF US CAN CHOOSE. TO DECIDE, I SUGGEST WE COUNT THE VULTURES WE SEE. THE ONE WITH THE MOST SIGHTINGS WINS.

VERY WELL.

AT THE END OF THE DAY, REMUS SAYS HE HAS SEEN SIX VULTURES.

HA! I HAVE SEEN TWELVE. SO, I CHOOSE THE HILL.

TWELVE? I DON'T BELIEVE YOU.

IN ANGER, ROMULUS TURNS HIS BACK ON HIS BROTHER...

I WILL BUILD THE CITY ON THE PALATINE HILL. YOU CAN JOIN ME OR YOU CAN WATCH!!

LATER...

IS THAT THE BEST YOU CAN DO? I COULD JUMP OVER THIS WALL...

THAT WOULD BE INVADING YOUR CITY. AND **THAT** WOULD MEAN DEATH TO THE INVADER!!!

HA, HA, HA, HA, HA,

SHHLLING

HORATIUS AND THE BRIDGE

IN 510 BC, THE ROMANS EXPELLED KING TARQUIN THE PROUD. LARS PORSENA, THE ETRUSCAN LEADER, DECIDED TO MAKE ROME PAY FOR THIS INSULT. HE GATHERED AN ARMY OF 90,000 MEN AND MARCHED ON ROME.

HORATIUS COCLES IS ON GUARD DUTY AT THE BRIDGE OVER THE TIBER. SUDDENLY, THE ETRUSCANS APPEAR ON THE JANICULUM HILL OPPOSITE...

IF THEY CAPTURE THIS BRIDGE, ROME WILL BE LOST.

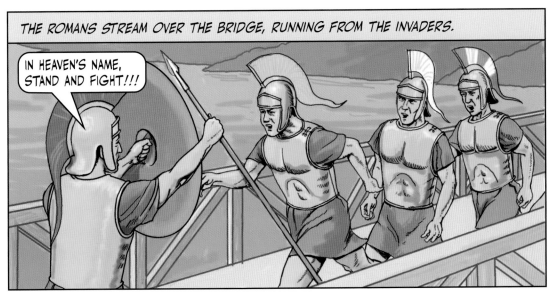

THE ROMANS STREAM OVER THE BRIDGE, RUNNING FROM THE INVADERS.

IN HEAVEN'S NAME, STAND AND FIGHT!!!

BUT NO ONE STOPS... THEN HORATIUS REALIZES HE MUST DO SOMETHING.

YOU MUST BREAK DOWN THE BRIDGE. I WILL HOLD OFF THE ETRUSCANS.

TWO SOLDIERS – SPURIUS LARTIUS AND TITUS HERMINIUS – FEEL GUILTY LETTING HORATIUS FACE THE ENEMY ALONE.

WE WILL JOIN YOU, HORATIUS.

THE THREE ROMANS STRUGGLE AGAINST THE HUGE ETRUSCAN ARMY. BUT THEY MANAGE TO STOP THE INVADERS' ADVANCE.

THE FIGHTING IS FIERCE. BODIES BEGIN TO PILE UP IN FRONT OF THE THREE MEN.

WHEN ONLY A SMALL PART OF THE BRIDGE IS LEFT, SPURIUS AND TITUS RUN BACK TO THE OTHER SIDE.

WHERE IS HORATIUS?

HE IS STILL FIGHTING.

SUDDENLY, THE REST OF THE BRIDGE COLLAPSES!!! HORATIUS IS TRAPPED ON THE WRONG SIDE!!!

KERRRACK

HORATIUS PRAYS TO THE RIVER...

TIBERNIUS, HOLY FATHER, I PRAY THAT YOU WILL TAKE THIS ARMOR AND THIS WARRIOR INTO YOUR STREAM.

HE DIVES INTO THE RIVER WEARING HIS HEAVY ARMOR.

MIRACULOUSLY, HE SURFACES AND SWIMS FOR THE BANK.

HURRAH!!
HURRAH!!
HURRAH!!

THUS, ROME IS SAVED. FOR HIS BRAVE DEEDS, HORATIUS IS REWARDED WITH LAND AND A STATUE OF HIM IS BUILT IN ROME.

HORATIUS COCLES

THE END

MORE MYTHICAL CHARACTERS

Most of the Roman gods and myths were borrowed from the ancient Greeks after the Romans conquered them in the second century BC. However, there were many characters from myths and legends that only appeared in Roman stories.

BELLONA – A goddess of war.

FAUNA – The wife of Faunus who was worshipped as the goddess of the fields and earth.

FAUNUS – The grandson of Saturn who was worshipped as the god of fields and shepherds. He was also the god of fortune telling. He had the head and body of a man, and the legs of a goat. A form of his name, Fauns, is used to describe similar creatures that lived in the countryside.

FLORA – The goddess of flowers. She was always youthful and there was a festival to honor her in the spring and bring on a good harvest.

GENIUS – A man's spirit. The Romans believed that every man had his own Genius who would protect him throughout his life. On their birthdays, men gave presents to their Genius.

JANUS – The porter of heaven and the month January is named after him. He is the guardian of gates and is shown as having two heads because every doorway faces two ways. There were many temples in Rome that were built for worshipping Janus.

JUNO – A woman's spirit. The Romans believed that every woman had her own Genius who would protect her throughout her life. On their birthdays, women gave presents to their Genius.

LARES – These were house gods. They were believed to be the souls of the dead ancestors of the household who were supposed to watch over and protect the living members.

LUCINA – The goddess of childbirth.

MITHRAS – A Persian god who was popular with Romans after they conquered the eastern Mediterranean. Mithras is often shown killing a bull with an axe. Bull sacrifice was a central part of worship. Women were not allowed to attend these ceremonies.

PALES – The goddess of cows and fields.

PENATES – Gods who looked after the house. Their name comes from Penus, meaning the pantry, where food was kept. Every home had a master who was the priest of the penates.

POMONA – A goddess who looked after fruit trees.

QUIRINUS – A war god. He was said to be Romulus, founder of Rome, who was made a god after his death.

SATURN – A Roman god. Some say that he was the Greek god Cronos, who was sent away from heaven by Jupiter, and went to Italy. The feast of Saturnalia was held every year in the winter. At the feast, no work was done and friends gave presents to each other. Slaves sat at their own table and were served by their masters. This showed that all people were the same in Saturn's world.

TERMINUS – The god of landmarks. His statues were rough stones or posts, set in the ground to mark a boundary or end of a field.

VESTA – The goddess of the hearth (fireplace). A holy fire was kept alight in her temple by six pure priestesses called vestals.

GLOSSARY

ancestors Distant relatives, who are farther back than grandparents.

bough A large branch from a tree.

conquer To defeat another land using weapons.

destiny Things that will happen in the future that are beyond control.

Etruscans A civilization that ruled most of Italy before the Romans.

expelled Being officially sent away from a place as a punishment.

grief Deep suffering, often at the loss of something or someone.

grove A small group of trees.

harpies Vicious and nasty winged monsters with the head and body of a woman, and the tail, wings, and claws of a bird.

incense A material that is burned to make a strong, pleasant smell.

oracle Someone who is considered to be very wise and can predict the future. An oracle can also talk with the gods.

Persians People from the country of Persia, now Iran.

Polydorus The youngest son of Hecuba and Priam, king of Troy. He was murdered by Polymestor, king of Thrace.

priestess A woman who oversees religious ceremonies.

prophetess A woman who can communicate with the gods.

quest A search for something.

revenge To get even with someone who has hurt you by doing something unpleasant back to the person.

River Styx The main river in the underworld.

sacred When something is set apart as religious or holy.

sibyl A female guide to the underworld.

siege When an army surrounds a city and does not let in supplies of food or water until the city surrenders.

spirits Ghostly beings.

superstition A fear of the unknown or of religion or magic.

Trojan horse A huge wooden horse left as a gift for Troy by the Greeks. When the Trojans brought it into the city, the Greeks jumped out from inside the horse and took over the city.

underworld The world of the dead, which is underneath the world of the living.

vultures Large birds of prey that eat the bodies of dead animals.

worship Ceremonies and prayers dedicated to a god or gods.

FOR MORE INFORMATION

ORGANIZATIONS

Fine Arts Museums of San Francisco
Legion of Honor
34th Avenue & Clement Street
Lincoln Park
San Francisco, CA 94121
(415) 750-3600
Web site: http://www.thinker.org/legion

J. Paul Getty Museum
1200 Getty Center Drive
Los Angeles, CA 90049-1687
(310) 440-7330
Web site: http://www.getty.edu/museum

The Metropolitan Museum of Art
1000 Fifth Avenue
New York, NY 10028-0198
(212) 535-7710
Web site: http://www.metmuseum.org

FOR FURTHER READING

Burrell, Roy. *First Ancient History*. New York, NY: Oxford University Press, Inc., 1999.

Kingfisher. *Mythology: Gods, Goddesses and Heroes from Around the World*. London, England: Kingfisher Publications Plc., 2001.

Philip, Neil. *The Illustrated Book of Myth*. London, England: Dorling Kindersley, Penguin Group, 1995.

Ross, Stewart. *The Best Tales Ever Told: Warriors and Witches*. New York, NY: Copper Beech Books, 1997.

INDEX

Web Sites

Due to the changing nature of Internet links, the Rosen Publishing Group, Inc., has developed an online list of Web sites related to the subject of this book. This site is updated regularly. Please use this link to access the list:

http://www.rosenlinks.com/gm/roman